Something to Think About

Something to Think About

A Grandmother
&
Granddaughter's
Poetry

For Valerie ~ Enjoy!

Louise A. Hess

Louise A. Hess

&

Jennifer E. Hess

J. E. Hess

Published by
Dog Ear Publishing
4010 W. 86th Street, Ste H
Indianapolis, IN 46268

www.dogearpublishing.net

ISBN: 978-145753-461-4
This book is printed on acid-free paper.

Printed in the United States of America

This book is dedicated to

grandmothers and granddaughters everywhere,

and to the special bond they share.

We have stopped for a moment to encounter each other, to meet, to love, to share. This is a precious moment, but it is transient. It is a little parenthesis in eternity. If we share with caring, lightheartedness, and love, we will create abundance and joy for each other, and then this moment will have been worthwhile.

Deepok Chopra

The Seven Spiritual Laws of Success

ACKNOWLEDGEMENTS

I thank my granddaughter, Jennifer Elizabeth Hess, for readily agreeing to co-author this book of poetry. This project was truly a labor of love. Being her grandmother and watching her blossom into a fine person and a poet, has been wonderfully pleasant and exceedingly gratifying. *L*

Although he professes not to understand poetry, I thank my husband, Bill Hess, for reading the manuscript and offering feedback on style and content. I thank him for doing the original sketches of the cover and chapter pages. I so appreciate his interest in all my work. *L*

I thank my grandmother, Louise Ann Hess, for introducing me to writing and instilling a love of poetry into my heart. Without her constant encouragement and feedback, I may never have been able to write the poems to complete my part of this book. *J*

I thank my parents, Bill and Deb Hess, for supporting my love of writing and providing feedback on the poems they read. I thank my boyfriend, Zac Kostenko, for his support throughout the process of completing this book. *J*

We thank Becky Edlebrock, Margaret Winn, and Susan Sterner for reading the manuscript and for their constructive commentary. *LJ*

We thank our editor, Lisa Wroble, for her editing, insightful suggestions, and encouragement for our project. *LJ*

The following poems have been previously published:

"Dreams" £J *Apple Blossom Time: An Autobiography in Prose and Poetry* 2011; and INTERACTIONS Family Newsletter, August 2001.

"Coffee Shop" and "Dark Lullaby" *J The Lance*, Worcester Academy Literary Review, Spring 2005.

"Snow" *J* and "Snowflake"£ INTERACTIONS Hess Family Newsletter, January 2001.

"Spider" £ PERSPECTIVES 4, Annual College of Mount St. Joseph Literary Journal, 1990.

"The Magic Box" £ INTERACTIONS Hess Family Newsletter, December 1999.

"The Juggler"£ INTERACTIONS Hess Family Newsletter, February 2002.

TABLE OF CONTENTS

PREFACE

Although *Something to Think About* is a book of poetry, it didn't start out that way. The events leading up to the format of the book started in June 2003, when I asked my then seventeen-year-old granddaughter, Jennifer Hess, if she would like to collaborate with me on a book of prose and poetry. She quickly responded that she'd love to do this project. You might ask, "Why would you want to write a book with a teenager?" The answer is simple; that particular teenager loves the written word as much as I do. We are both avid readers and we are both committed to developing our writing skills. In addition, each of us has already published some of our work and we work together as editor and assistant editor for our family newsletter *INTERACTIONS: Hess Family News & Views.* But most important of all is the fact that we had already co-authored a few poems and stories and enjoyed the process. We did it just for fun and the pure joy of playing with words. Collaborating on a book would be another way to enhance our already fine relationship.

At first, we brainstormed through e-mails and phone calls. Later on, we met to discuss subjects, plans, and timeline. We agreed on a five-year plan, with Jen's first priority to her schoolwork. She did that, thus completing high school and college with honors. She is now focused on her new career in consulting for a large company in the Washington D.C. area; so we revised our timeline.

Once we settled on a theme, format, and title, we discussed cover art. We tossed around all sorts of designs, fonts, and images. When Jen suggested using the greater than symbol, we knew immediately that it was perfect for us in that it expressed our combined efforts. It seemed too simple, so I suggested intersecting the symbol with vertical lines denoting the four parts of our book: Different, Similar, Same, and Together. We agreed. I enlisted my husband Bill to resurrect his drafting skills and do rough sketches of this idea for us to submit to the book cover designers when we had a finished manuscript.

We started compiling samples of our work. Then we identified specific areas and topics to address each in our own way. Jen and I listed subjects and divided them into four specific areas for the chapters:

Different: We each wrote about different subjects or areas of interest and used different styles of poetry.

Similar: We addressed similar topics like favorite color, nature, or music from the perspective of making music and hearing music.

Same: We selected fruit and to our amazement, we both wrote about peaches, we both did a poetry exercise called "The Magic Box," and wrote other *same* themes.

Together: We wrote specific poems together using a formula that has worked well for us in the past. For the poetry, we each wrote one line and e-mailed it to the other back and forth until we had something we both liked, then rearranged the lines as needed. For the story, one wrote a short paragraph or a few sentences and the other one picked up and continued the thought or took it in an entirely different direction.

Finding time is always a challenge. This book was a part-time endeavor for both of us. Ten years flew by. Many times our book project went on the back burner out of necessity or time constraints. I was heavily involved in completing our family cookbook: *Something Yummy: Treasured Family Recipes,* as well as immersed in the manuscript of my autobiography: *Apple Blossom Time: An Autobiography in Prose and Poetry.* During those years, my husband and I purchased a condo in Florida and quickly became acquainted with the fury of several hurricanes and all that they involved, as well as having a home for sale in Ohio during one of the worst times in real estate history. I also had major health issues and intense treatments that restricted my time and energy for a few years. That experience prompted me to get these writing projects completed in a timely manner. Nevertheless, I work best when I have deadlines to meet. In the ensuing years, I finished *Bouquet,* which is a book of fiction short stories. I am nearing completion of *The Power of Ten,* which is my memoir and part of our family history documents.

Jen and I met once or twice a year to review our progress, but did most of the work via e-mails. We used file folders; as they filled, we transferred to loose leaf binders. There were months when we didn't work on *Something to Think About* at all when life and other obstacles took precedence over this project; like when Jen had surgery and physical therapy for a major knee injury. But we always knew the book was important to us and never gave up. Although this book project is a natural extension of our established pattern of enjoyment, it was also an exercise in patience, perseverance, and grace. I knew I would gently prod her along until it was completed.

The hardest thing was deciding which pieces to cut or to change. It's difficult to edit your own work. Therefore, it's good to have a collaborator and review each other's work before getting a professional editor. Since I had more discretionary time, I offered to type the manuscript and find a publisher.

In mid-2011, I suggested that we revise our plans and we agreed to have 25 prose and 25 poetry selections each, which was a more manageable project for us. We devised a way our readers could identify our work without putting our names on each piece. A calligraphy letter $\mathcal{L}$ or $\mathcal{J}$ after the final punctuation worked well for us. We also used that in the *Table of Contents* to denote which pieces belong to Louise, Jen, or both of us.

At some point in early 2012, it became obvious to me that Jen preferred writing poetry. After prayer and reflection, I suggested to her that we change the content of our book to all poetry. She loved that idea, and I'm happy I figured it out. We decided to save the completed prose pieces for another project. A few of mine will be in *Random Thoughts by the Sea,* a non-fiction book of prose that's somewhat a continuation of *Apple Blossom Time.*

Although I write prose, I also enjoy writing poetry. Miss Smith, my high school sophomore English teacher, introduced me to the Romantic Age of Poetry and the works of Keats, Byron, and Shelley. Later on, my first steady boyfriend, Mike, wrote poetry for me. Therefore, from age fourteen on, I was hooked. I didn't start writing poetry until I was sixteen; but it was the typical love poetry of a teen. More than three decades went by before I started writing prose and poetry. Now I enjoy the discipline of haiku poetry, and have fun writing light, sometimes silly, poems as well as poetry with metaphor, or poetry that has a sub-text, or poetry that leaves the reader with food for thought.

The one hundred poems in *Something to Think About* have no central theme; they are both fiction and non-fiction. Some rhyme, others are prose poems, but most are free verse. A prose poem captures the essence of the topic incorporating all five senses, in one brief, descriptive paragraph.

I had a wonderful grandmother; her wisdom and love inspired me to develop special relationships with each of my grandchildren. She was my role model for my grandmothering. I believe Jen and I have a special connection and a fine relationship. We hope you enjoy reading *Something to Think About*, and we hope it gives *you* something to think about. It was a fun project for both of us—and a learning experience as well. We encourage you to get to know your grandparent/grandchild on a more personal level. Find a common bond like traveling, collecting, gardening, antiquing, or cooking; the areas of interest are limitless. We guarantee that you will be delighted with what you learn about each other, and we know it will enrich your lives. *L*

INTRODUCTION

Long before I could spell or write, I remember my grandmother sitting down and telling me a story and then asking me to tell *her* one. When I started writing, we sometimes compiled a list of random nouns, verbs, and adjectives and then she told me to use them in my story. Other times, we would write alternate lines. Sometimes I just started talking and let my young mind wander, and in time, that evolved into a creative piece. Whatever the method, this was where my love of writing started. As I grew, so did the stories. I took classes in creative writing and eagerly showed my grandma what I wrote. I submitted my work to my high school literary journal and was excited when I saw my first poem published. That's when I started to imagine what it would be like to actually publish my own book.

When I was in high school, my grandmother asked me if I would like to work on a book of prose and poetry with her. I said yes without hesitation. During my high school years, I wrote at least one poem a day, and made it a habit to write something before I went to sleep each night. Poetry was my outlet. Poetry was my voice.

Even during that phase, I was convinced that I was a short fiction writer. However, after my first creative writing college class, where one-half of the term focused on short stories and the other half on poetry, I knew that poetry was my favorite genre. From then on, I took class after class to hone my skills and learn to think outside the box. Although I have been told that my poems read like prose, I find that this is the way I can best express myself.

While sharing our works with each other, I could instantly see how my grandma and I were similar and different. She loves prose and writes in this form more than I do. Since I did not gravitate toward prose, we decided that this would be a book of poetry. I also saw that my grandma was sometimes literal whereas I liked to be more figurative with my poetry. Yet despite these differences, our minds were usually in the same place. This is what prompted the chapters in our book.

The themes for the chapters are in themselves revealing. Not only does the *Different* chapter show different topics of interest from two different age perspectives, but also the *Similar* and *Same* chapters depict how the same situation or object can be observed and told in other ways. *Together* shows just how magical it can be when those two mindsets can come together as one to create something truly amazing.

Isn't that the beauty in the written word? I look at a cloud and write about dragons and rabbits, you look at the same cloud and see cotton balls and smoke. It's all what we perceive and how our minds function. I hope this is something you can take with you after reading *Something to Think About*. I also hope this book helps you to think more about your perspective on life. *J*

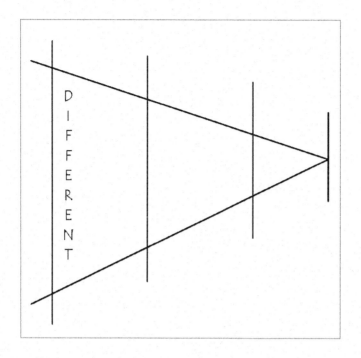

DIFFERENT covers widely diverse, mundane subjects like peas and patience. It also addresses self-reliance in "Her Day" and "Strength," and emotional themes like love in "Trip, Stumble, Fall," "Comfort," and "Love Sonnet." We wrote about descriptive topics like "Through the Beaded Curtain" and "The Sunday Newspaper," as well as fanciful topics like "The Juggler" and "Natural Brilliance." There are poems about loss in "Beginning of the End," and about good advice in "A Way of Life" and "A Perfect Day." Don't be alarmed by the fonts in "Whine – Wine," they are not typos; they are there to simply denote chaos. This was the easiest chapter and it is the longest chapter with forty poems because it allowed greater freedom in selecting our own subjects. This fun chapter allowed us to experiment with unusual topics and different styles of writing. ℒ

Her Day

Nothing was the same
now that it was morning.
She held her life
in her hands
as if it were a prism
emitting dancing rainbows.
Her inner glow like the
sun awakening a new day.
Her passion like red wildflowers
searing the edges of meadows
when they meet
the undulating seas.
She reflected on crystal clear
moments in her life.
The life she now
held in her hands,
and nothing was the same
now that it was the
dawning of *her* day. £

Trip, Stumble, Fall

Ocean blue eyes
call my name.
You notice me.
I will not fall.
Slowly we talk,
become closer,
you're just a friend.
I try not to fall.
Turn away,
pain awaits,
you don't like me.
I stumble.
Summer comes;
we're together more.
I find you amazing.
I slowly fall.
I hear you like me;
think it's a lie,
it can't be true.
I'm falling.
We go out,
it seems a dream.
Happiness rises
Too late!
Treat me well,
don't leave me.
I'm so addicted.
I fell. J

Behind the Beaded Curtain

A tiny bell jingles
like on a cat's collar
as I stroll through the door.
Incense invigorates my senses
making it almost impossible
to distinguish between
musk blended with rose
and a faint hint of nutmeg.

A portly woman in black
saunters out and grasps my hand.
Bracelets circle up and down
both forearms—
no one would ever misplace her
with constant clinking
of metal on metal.
She escorts me
behind a beaded curtain
obscuring a barely visible future.

The room shrouds clarity,
I ease myself onto a red plush chair.
Candles speckle the countertop
like a reverse Dalmatian,
emanating a muted glow.
My palms throw a fit;
my nerves jump rope within me.

A blue velvet canopy soars
with a flick of her wrist
and jangle of bracelets.
The clear orb looks like a giant eye

filled with numerous grey pupils
that appear to be studying me;
tallying my faults
as I take heed of the dust that lies
on its black lacquered foot.

I glimpse my reflection
in the glassy surface before me.
As I settle back into my seat,
I notice a hairline fracture
on the otherwise unblemished surface. *J*

Order

Although there is order in disorder,
her rage could no longer be contained.
Her self-imposed solitude
shielded her from pain
from hungering for love
from a merciless foe.
When will she be at peace?
When will this war end?
If history is repeated
there is no justice
for the common person.
Ecstasy is reserved for the angels,
gratitude is often feigned,
grace becomes acquiescence. £

The Housing Crisis

"We are the lives of houses when no one else is there."
-Realtor

A home returning from the absence
of an owner is a welcoming scent

wrapped in a warm embrace.
And though I ponder, question

and debate the defining
points of a residence, abode,

and what it changes in us—feet
kicked back, hearts eased

as if to relax minds or have meaning
hidden in potpourri—I remind myself,

It's okay to be nearsighted. It's okay to acknowledge
how the home felt, shared

warmth, hosted parties, opened
itself to the owner who never returned. *J*

One Pea

One pea in a pod,
indistinguishable in color
from the pod and other peas.
Symmetrically formed orbs
aligned in a row.
Graduated sizes like
a string of mini green pearls.
Tasty morsels, raw or cooked
bits of nature.

Upon closer inspection,
one pea is different;
larger, fuller than the others.
In its central position,
clearly unlike the last ones
toward the tapered ends
of the pod—those flat,
ill-formed, immature peas.

The full, round, mature pea
is ripe, bursting with life,
ready to send out
curved white buds
of stem and root
hidden just beneath its skin.
Perhaps one day away
from bursting out of its casing
in its search for light and soil
that ensures propagation
to sustain life everlasting.

Oh, to be part of the promise of tomorrow! £

Natural Brilliance

I am a piece of white bread;
nothing special to look at,
and so common I may be
overlooked.
Unlike my rye and wheat cousins,
I must dress myself up
to catch your attention
(because I am not naturally brilliant).
Would you prefer I be toasted?
Perhaps that would add the sass
you desire, but I will still be
rough around the edges;
sever my crust from my body
for a disjointed texture.
You can decorate me—
use peanut butter and jelly
for a more American flair,
or perhaps some honey
to sweeten your perception.
I may not be unique
like pumpernickel
or strangely pleasing
like sourdough,
but don't misinterpret my bleached exterior
with boredom.
I will convince you
through versatility
that I, too, can achieve greatness. *J*

Someday, Sometime

Some days I just want to fly away. Over the clouds of black and across the sea of rage. Around the threatening sands and through the mystical forests. Sometimes I want to rid myself of these chains that bind me to my past. Sometimes I wish that I could snap my fingers and instantly become the person I wish to be. I wish it were that easy. Alas— there are mountains we must ascend and each step brings us closer to our goal. Remember—mountains form over time. There will forever be obstacles in our way. Blocking our paths; smearing our dreams, dwindling our hopes. *J*

A Way of Life

Worries plague everyone
one time or another,
causing angst, grief,
indigestion, and
frown lines.
"Don't worry,"
seems flippant advice.
If it were that easy
we'd all be smiling,
whistling, maybe even
hop, skip, and jumping.
But it isn't.
What is one to do?
Stay positive.
Learn to see the
glass half-full.
Keep trying;
soon it will be a habit,
then a way of life. £

Claddagh

Friendship
Love
Loyalty
when combined
create the claddagh.
This symbol,
though small,
means something great.

Friendship:
A key facet in one's life.
Friends are needed
to celebrate
joys and sorrows;
laughter and tears.

Love:
From friendship,
love may blossom.
In a relationship,
you must be sure
that the love is
backed by friendship.

Loyalty:
A component necessary
in all the others
Especially love.
One cannot have a
successful relationship
without loyalty.

All these concepts
build on each other,
creating an intricate
connection and meaning.
The claddagh is
one symbol,
one meaning,
one promise. *J*

Analysis of a Prolonged Chase
To Wile E. Coyote

Never have I seen
someone as dedicated as you,
though your reasoning
confounds me. If you ask me,
it's not like the roadrunner
is a filling main course –
more like an appetizer.
But what is he preceding?
And I recommend you stop
using Acme products. They obviously
fail – where do you get the money
for them anyways? If you can pay
for rockets and anvils, you can pay
for a meal at a diner.
I'm astonished
you haven't starved yet
since you never seem to eat
and only constantly pursue.
Perhaps this failed chase
is on purpose;
perhaps you are a vegetarian
in denial.
What will you do with your life,
Mr. Coyote, when you finally catch
your elusive rival? Who will you
cry to in despair? *J*

Trying to Write with an Uncreative Mind
Inspired by "Stopping By the Woods on a Snowy Evening"
by Robert Frost

Whose words these are I feel I know.
My pen is on the table, though;
I will not cease to stay on guard
To write my words in steady flow.

My silent mind does find it hard
To write without some kind of bard
Between the sights and thoughts that weigh
The darkest moments leave us scarred.

I throw my paper ball away—
The words were flowing in cliché.
The only other sound's the tap
My pen will make throughout the day.

The words are lost inside a trap,
But I have episodes of gaps,
And sometimes poems fall in my lap,
And sometimes poems fall in my lap. *J*

The Coffee Shop

I glance up from my book of fantasy. The delicate aroma of coffee and pastries surrounds me as I take another sip of my hazelnut coffee with three scoops of sugar and a dash of cream. I see a happy couple walk in. I hear the guy behind me ask his date out followed by her enthusiastic yes. The man to my right is ordering a dozen roses on his cell phone for his wife's birthday. I take another sip of coffee and return to my book. I imagine myself as the main character who's involved in so many adventures and always seems to get the sweetest boyfriends. At least I can escape into my fantasy world, even if it is for only a brief moment. For now, the server who gives me my daily caffeine fix can be my love. Coffee substitutes flowers. A cheese danish—some jewelry (a delicious treat sometimes added to spice things up). I give him a flirty smile and ask for a refill. After, I continue with my book as he yet again fades into the background—along with the rest of the world. *J*

Patience

Await an hour
as time stands still.
Each breath an eternity,
each second a decade.

Await a moment
that stretches to the horizon.
Fanciful dreams override
doubts of coming true.

Await a word
that is just beyond memory.
Others fight for your attention
while the golden one is unattainable.

Await a thought
when the spark is gone.
The minutes mock,
the silence is deafening. *J*

Whine - Wine

Murphy's Law was running wild,

A *BAD* hair day as well,

burned the roast beyond recognition,

set off the smoke detectors,

neighbors came running,

fire engines with sirens blaring,

kids fighting, TV droning, dog barking,

fish tank *l e a k i n g,*

A/C conked o u t, guests due in an hour,

table arrangement wilting,

tears sting my eyes,

whine, whine, whine,

another day in happily ever after!

Please pass the wine. £

Comfort

A wooden path,
to a seaside retreat,
impelling as a siren's call.
Sea treasures tumbling to the beach,
graceful shore birds gliding
on air currents,
wing-tipped manta rays
waving at each other.
Sand and sea
my unbeatable de-stressors.
Here I welcome
random thoughts,
fleeting wishes,
comfort food,
and urgent kisses.
Laughing, living, loving,
listening, learning.
And etched forever
on my heart
is the depth of my love
for you, Bill.
And yes, my heart
still skips a beat
when you enter the room. £

Dark Lullaby

run
far away
to the land of no end
where the sky is black
the stars shine bright
and the moon is always full

dance
in circles
to the song of the wind
that urges you to surrender
with its sweet caress
causing worries to be forgotten

whisper
of love
and of the future and past
that remains bound to us
for all eternity
when all else comes crashing down ♩

The World Through a Raindrop

How a raindrop
may dive and impact
your skin – a release of
kinetic energy, a bead
of hand-blown glass –
and make one feel
rejuvenated and renewed.
Whatever the drop,
perhaps snow or gumdrop,
any liquid you have shed
or felt – it enlivens your spirit
to see yellows and oranges.

Pretend you live within this drop
and see the world askew through
dew – refracting reality.
Outside this globule,
the world is clear to the eye
but it isn't quite authentic;
you need glasses to see the fine print. *J*

Sunday Newspaper

The Sunday newspaper,
five pounds of annoyance.
Ads, coupons, inserts are a part,
as are comics, puzzles, weather.
Real estate section is half of it,
automotive, business, arts,
another part, leaving
less than ten pages of news.
Some isn't really news,
just Hollywood drivel,
crime reports, obits,
business deals, stock forecasts,
rehashed political scandals,
and international chaos.
Why do I buy newspapers?
I don't need them to start a fire,
or line the canary cage, or
protect floors when painting.
Yet whenever they
fail to deliver it,
I am so disappointed,
my day incomplete.
I miss my smudged fingers,
the smell of newsprint,
the hot off the press
aura of news.
I do not like a
paperless existence,
some things cannot be
held in clouds. £

Have a Sensory Christmas

See lovely sights of beribboned gifts, glittering trees,
twinkling lights, tables set with candles, cloudless star-
filled skies, smiling faces, bright eyes.

Look at Christmas visions of delight.

Smell luscious aromas of roasts, cookies, chestnuts, mulled
wine, pine boughs, white roses, cedar logs, crisp winter air.

Inhale Christmas perfume of goodness.

Touch pleasing textures of velvet vests, satin trims, furry
hats, woolen mittens, Santa's beard, blanketing
snowflakes, warm breath.

Feel Christmas caresses of love.

Taste splendid flavors of favorite foods, fruitcakes, hot
cocoa, eggnog, candy canes, gingerbread, a lover's gentle
kiss.

Savor Christmas sweetness of happiness.

Hear joyful sounds of Church bells, sleigh bells, holiday
toasts, a mellow sax, angelic flutes, carolers, choirs,
Hosannas of thanks.

Listen to Christmas music of memories. £

Strength

The succession of gardens
in my life marks rites of passage
from external realities
to my inner self.
They showed me the way
when I was immersed in silence.
Lilac perfumed breezes
inspired me to celebrate
the music of my soul and
rhythms of my life.
The whistling winds
kept my spirit buoyant
as I received the penetrating
light of healing,
like the sun uncovering
hidden places.
In a dreamlike walk through
the inner garden of my mind,
I found refuge in my secret self.
I was nourished and sustained
by the abundance of love,
and delighted in the hidden source
of my strength that
constantly restores me
as needed. £

The Juggler

He starts out slowly with
just one or two.
When that's going well,
he adds Sara and Sue.
I wonder how he
keeps them in line.
What? He now has nine!
He's amazing, he's focused,
he's a daredevil too.
One of these days
he may drop a few and
some may even
bid him *adieu*.
But for now he keeps
practicing to fine-tune his skill.
As he juggles his women,
hats off to our Bill. £

In Limbo

1. Without Judgment
To die without judgment
is to reach to the stars
on a falling iron chain.

2. A Vulture Circles Above The Desert
It awaits its dying dinner
on china plates,
on a bed of beetle shells,
on final prayers.

3. Purgatory
It is overcast in Purgatory.
Hazy trees offer limbs of regret,
the sun shines occasionally between clouds,
the rain falls in darkness
like ghosts in painful memories.
Eternity evaluates from the shadows.

4. Dream
When sound asleep,
a dream of economic delight creeps –
the illusion of waking hours.

5. Hope
Hope cements the faces of the unjudged
in limbo.
Sufferers, fold your hands,
disregard your lying truths
of candied politics,
and stray from ultimate answers.

The afterlife
offers no promises.

6. **Intermission in Shakespeare**
A time to speculate the end
of unresolved plot
and budding resolutions.
Which is the ideal solution?

7. **The Original Sin**
In the unforgettable garden,
ivory swans swim
without grace.
A crimson apple is plucked
to please, to enlighten:
Eve is only a day
before the real tragedy;
a dam of intellect.
The garden fell to desire.

8. **Results**
Healthy answers don't appear;
they extend.
In clinical studies
only results cradle patience.

9. **Death In Limbo**
Time eternalizes at death.
Pending residency
prolongs the mind's insanity –
a convicting damnation. *J*

I Want To Cry

I want to cry when it rains
if it's important enough
for the clouds to cry—
so will I.
I want to cry when babies do,
they voice their unhappiness,
without hesitation—
so will I.
I want to cry when a dove does,
as it coos and calls
for its mate—
so will I.
I want to cry when I cry
even when there's
no apparent reason why—
I will cry. £

Love Sonnet

My love is an ocean teaming with life
ever-changing yet always a delight.
It is my solace, my haven from strife.
Sometimes roaring, sometimes still as night.
I love the white capped cresting waves and sea foam,
as the restless sea hugs the waiting shore,
calming sounds and salty scents call me home
the way it will forever more.
The ever-present tidal ebb and flow
relying on phases of the moon.
Despite stormy weather this much I know,
seashells entangled in roots along the dunes.
My love is a sea, deep and truly blue.
With one wish, I'd wish an ocean for you. £

First Sight

Lights dim low
    smoky haze
sound of ivory
    followed by bass.
Bodies sway
    laced fingers touch
whispers in ears
    silence hushed.
Dancers part
    follow the line
across the room
    eyes that bind.
A smile creeps
    look away
glance back over
    unwavering gaze.
Cross the room
    steady pace
introductions made
    this is fate. *J*

Not Yet

Not yet.
I am not ready.
The days are long,
but not long enough.
The hours slip
through my fingers
The urgency ever-present.
The need an ache within.
Goals attainable
as they should be.
Yet I must make them happen.
But not yet.
I am not ready.

I will know when I am. $\mathcal{L}$

Moonlight Warnings

What would happen if the moon
could speak of the night – of what
happens in the world when there is
no light, and the innocent sleep?
Would we be warned
of danger in the darkness?
Would we choose to ignore – continue
to sleep with pleasant dreams
oblivious of shadowed tragedies?

Each month, she tries to reach
out. Each new moon begins the cycle –
growing bright with confidence until
she reaches her pinnacle and shouts:

Listen to tragedies
worse than Greek plays.
Don't close your ears
harm is coming your way.

No one listens
and she fades to darkness.
Her faith in mankind vanishing.
But each night she rises –
observing those snuggled under covers
unaware of perils.
If only we would look up
and listen
to hear her cries. *J*

Soul Window

I gaze into the soul window
and what do I see?
Twinkling lights shining,
content as can be.
The house looks so peaceful,
the sun shining bright,
from this house I see
the world in new light.

I gaze into the soul window
and what do I see?
Tears of rain falling,
but could it be with glee?
To discover answers
one must console.
Though the clouds seem dark,
there may not be dole.

I gaze into the soul window
and what do I see?
The lights all burnt out,
the house looks dark to me.
I miss the light
that twinkled inside.
Light that always made
me stand with such pride. *J*

The Races

Good ol' Red, White, and Blue.
Dividing
identifying
grouping people.
There's an elephant
in the room
surrounded by asses.
Who stands out more?
Elephant has size
but is considered slow.
Donkeys are plentiful
and never stop braying
always a complaint
never satisfied.
Then again
the elephant isn't always
the better of the two.
If asked,
who would you choose?
Red with anger
blue with disbelief.
Divided votes
leading to a divided nation.
Always try to fit
the elephant and the donkey
into molds.
Must be exact –
discrepancies are not accepted.
Look one way
and get called out.
Look another and get shunned.
There is no indivisible land

if there are haters,
segregators
unacceptors.
Why can't I choose
a polar bear?
There is no success if there are only two options.
Remove the labels
and vote for the country. *J*

Elegant Lady

She stands alone
in the jet-black harbor
surrounded by twinkling
city jewels
sometimes almost halo-like.
Wonderfully inspiring,
evoking countless stories,
a welcome committee of one,
but oh what an important one.
I look for her
whenever I fly into the City.
I'm happy she has always
been there to greet me.
Serene,
majestic,
stately,
elegant lady
symbol of freedom. £

Morning Delight

My eyes feasted
on a delicious breakfast delight
of a cloud strata.
Layers of gauzy white clouds
between tiers of blue sky,
muted, multi-shades of blue
like the tri-color yarn
my mother used to knit sweaters
and baby blankets.
Layers of clouds
dotted here and there with
sea gulls and copious amounts
of sunshine poured over all.
The deliciousness of the
summer sky sated my
need for beauty. £

Realizations

You always respected your dog
more than you respected me.
I will never understand
why. You never had to ask
me to come when you wished for
my company. I didn't need training
to give you the attention
and care that you wanted.
I didn't need to hear "good girl"
with a pat on the head
to know that I had done well
with the gifts I gave you.
I loyally stayed by your side
and didn't whimper in the corner
when you took your stress
and frustration out on me.
I was your most trustworthy companion,
yet your dog is sleeping by your side
while I stand alone in the rain.

Now I watch from your window
and I see you for what you are.
You charm your way into
the hearts of the unsuspecting;
supplying sweet words after slashing
jagged cuts with your tongue.
You had me playing tricks,
waiting for the treat I deserved:
(your undying love and loyalty
in return for mine).
You allowed me a taste
of your love, of your promises

for a future together,
and then had me on a leash.
Focusing on the bone
you dangled in front of my nose,
I didn't notice that your gaze
diverted away from me
until I was locked away
in the pound with other forgotten pets. _J_

Search for a New Beginning
A Response to the Three Gorges River Project

Tattered buildings surround
a work zone. Rubble creates
roads or sidewalks – it is hard
to tell what lies underneath.
Workers wear hard hats and dig.
They dig through cement
and plaster but never reach bottom.
Never finding what they are
looking for, whatever that is.
Others walk around in disbelief –
a week ago there was laughter
filling their abandoned homes.

Shattered windows trimmed
with bright blues and greens.
Doors broken off hinges, and yet
there are plants on crumbling balconies.
Some still green with life, others
fading to brown as if they must die
along with the buildings.
Why do these workers not rebuild
so residents can return to their homes
to care for their plants?
Instead, they stare at the ground as if
an answer – a reason – will surface
and lead them in the right direction.

Beyond this devastation is a hill –
a hill green with brilliance and beauty,
Red paint on white boards are posted,
looming over the destruction.

Chinese characters that the workers
can look up at and read. Do they say
hope – life – beginning – believe?
Or perhaps they are constant reminders
of grim conditions, orders to
work – forget – suffer – abandon.
Whatever the message,
the workers carry on
and the houses remain empty.

The excavating continues
while residents walk incredulously.
Everyone is looking for an answer.
The vibrant paint will soon begin to peel
leaving the homes
as lifeless as their surroundings –
lessening the chance of return.

One yellow hard hat
lies on the ground. Perhaps
that worker knew that what he was
looking for could not be found
under the perpetual pile of rubble. *J*

A Perfect Day

Celebrate each day for the gift it really is!
The sun is up and so am I.
That's blessing enough.
Dishwasher is broken
but repairman on his way.
Dark clouds above
but dry earth needs rain.
Kids in school and
the quiet is delicious.
The drone of raindrops
a welcome song.
A perfect day to write poetry.
A perfect day to meditate.
A perfect day to give thanks
for everything. *L*

How Sweet It Was

Sweet syrupy prose
as ridiculous as carrying
watermelons in a berry basket,
or catching butterflies on my tongue.

Sweet syrupy prose
so unlike me,
yet freeing me
to erratically fly away
to danceland
where I can step out onto
the darkened dance floor,
drape my train over my arm
as I go around and around
under dizzying mirrored lights.

Sweet syrupy prose
that should impede my progress
as I shrink smaller and smaller,
lost on a honey-coated dance floor,
a bee in a sugary sea
floating away into dreamland
where shooting stars
sound like silver bells.

The alarm clock rings and
the sweetness is gone. £

Morning Brew

The alarm buzzes to alert him that it is 4:45 a.m.
His hand bats around the table
until it rests on the familiar oval button
that offers him five more minutes.
Sitting up, he grumbles
about how he despises morning shifts
and rubs his cinched eyes to unlock
the sleep cage that imprisons them
in a world of fermented barley.

After stretching, he scratches his shoulder
and licks his parched lips.
He stumbles downstairs, the electronic coffee maker
already percolated the coffee,
and he inhales the bitter aroma
that permeates the kitchen.
But he staggers past and opens the refrigerator
to feel a cold blast of air
smack into his body — he fumbles inside
and grasps for a way to forget
the mundane living that keeps him hostage.
He plops down on the sofa,
brings the bottle to his lips,
and takes his first swig of the day.
A clock releases five chimes. *J*

Sisters

How do you define sunshine?
Bright, warm, beautiful?
And how do you define sisters?
Reliable, fun, cherished?
On some level,
they seem interchangeable.
When you realize the
similarities between sisters,
it is an astonishing,
yet comforting, thing.
And that's how it seems with you,
my dear sister-friend.
I treasure our friendship,
I treasure you,
as a very special person
in my life. £

Smile

She wants me to smile.
"Come on," she coaches.
But I cannot do that.
It would look fragile, false, feigned.
I am normally quick to laugh or cry.
My emotions, like my mind,
always in high gear.

Maybe there are smiles
left inside of me.
Surely there must be!
But where are they?
I need them to bubble up
spontaneously, through the chaos,
from the well of happiness
deep within me.
But I cannot access that well.
I cannot even cry.
So how can I smile
when I am in this limbo?

"Come on," she urges,
"Where's that beautiful smile?"
And sometimes it happens,
just a surface smile
that lacks eyes and heart.
Maybe it's just a grin.
But even that little bit helps
relieve the pressure.
For that nanosecond a
vestige of my spirit emerges.

How can I cling to that spirit
in this dire time?
I feel depleted, overwhelmed, weary.
Where has my inner strength gone?
How can I reclaim serenity?
So how can I smile in this turmoil?
Will I ever have peace of mind again?

Maybe a smile is a start.

Smile?

It if were only that simple. £

Through My Window

Long, white, lacy ruffles
on a dark shawl
flutter against the edge
of paleness.
A perfect touch on
a moonless night.
Stars brighten the sky
and in the velvety hush
of silence
there is peace. ℒ

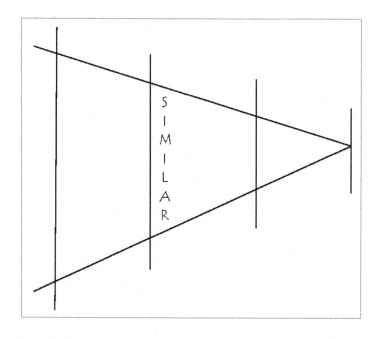

SIMILAR covers poems that are similar in subject such as our favorite colors, which are "Cranberry" and "Green and Purple," or the topic was nature and one wrote about "The Spider" and the other about "Rain." "The Airman" and "The Marine" are about service men we love. I, as a mother, wrote about "My Daughter;" Jen, as a daughter, wrote "My Mother." We both addressed learning and teaching in "The Spark" and "The Teacher;" my personal favorites in this book. When searching back files I found two poems, "Snow" and "Snowflake," that we wrote for our family newsletter 2001. We both address music and moving, and other topics as well. We enjoyed our similar discoveries all through the writing of this book. £

Spinner

Slowly,
patiently
the geometric orb weaver
creates her deceptive lacework,
then watches
and waits
in the central hub
for vibrations
signaling entrapment
and nourishment. £

Rain

I push my curtains aside and stare outside. Another dreary, rainy night. The damp smell from the outside enters my room as I open my window. Glistening droplets cling to the screen like a web. I run my fingers over the them, enjoying the cool refreshing feeling. I imagine myself standing in the street, letting the rain fall gently into my mouth, drinking in the moisture. I keep my window cracked as I get into bed and am lulled to sleep by the soothing impact of rain hitting the ground. *J*

Harmony

Study the music sheet –
rhythms beating.
Glance at notes.
Gentle pitch of a flute
emphasizes tenderness.
Screeching electric guitar
vents and releases energy.
Delicate tones of a piano
bring peace to life.
A chorus adds deeper meaning.
Communicate and
express music
however you please –
I choose instruments. *J*

Song of the City

Shrill whistles, droning motors,
deafening jack hammers, and
screeching brakes add to
the cacophony of horns, beeps,
and blasts of sound;
an unrehearsed song of the city.

People darting, rushing,
scurrying along to the
insistent pace set by
constant noise.
Airplanes roar overhead,
sirens on fire engines and
ambulances pierce
early morning hours;
music of the metropolis.

A discordant symphony
that plays on and on,
chorus after chorus.
It knows no reprieve and
gradually becomes unheard;
this endless song of the city. £

Cranberry

Ripe, rich, regal cranberry
my favorite color.
Other times in life
other colors were favored,
now vibrant yet mature
cranberry suits me to a tee.
As did the cranberry
mother-of-the-groom gown
with swirling chiffon pleats
so perfect for dancing.
A river of cranberry mums
fronts our home in Ohio,
reliable bloomers,
year after year,
armloads of flowers
to arrange and to give away.
Delicious tart cranberry sauce,
trendy cranberry martinis
challenge the taste buds.
If I had my dream car
it would definitely be a
cranberry Jaguar XL.
But for now,
I'm content with my
chocolate covered cranberries. *L*

Green and Purple

Green – the color of life,
vibrant and plentiful.
A sign of Spring,
of renewal
after a long frost.
Flavors of mint and basil
fill my mouth
and brightens meals.
A color of mystery;
green eyes are rare
and have always captivated
my attention.

Purple – a feminine color
that has swirled in
to my sea of green.
I used to avoid this hue
until I noticed
how vibrant it could be.
Violets and lilacs
complimented my foliage.
They began to dance
in perfect harmony;
winning over my love. *J*

The Marine

I have never seen him in uniform
but can tell by his behavior
that he is one of the few,
the Proud.
Meticulous cleaning,
everything in order
with no clutter in sight.
Disciplined workouts,
always pushing to the limits
and showing fortitude.
From discussing "battle rhythms"
when describing business
to finishing grand statements with
"Oorah Jenni? Oorah?"
I can see Devil Dog through and through.
Though he no longer serves,
his resilience and dedication are proved
with his Purple Heart.
Oh, how I would love to see him in uniform. *J*

The Airman

Shortly after we got engaged,
he enlisted, and left
after his 22nd birthday.
The need to serve his country
was more than a duty;
it was an honor and
a privilege he embraced.
I was proud of him,
but missed him beyond words.
Dozens of letters connected us,
I wrote long letters
often twice a day.
Calls were infrequent and brief,
the lines to use the phones
were always so long.
When he came home
on his first leave,
I didn't recognize him.
He was so thin,
his blond hair shorn,
the brimmed hat hid his face,
the long coat overpowered him,
but those dress blues
matched his eyes, and
my heart thundered.
The week flew by,
it tore me apart
to kiss him good-bye.
So many difficult good-byes
over the years,
but the returns
were always delicious. £

The Shells of Life

Crash of waves
    tumble shards of shells
        along granules of sand
            that sizzle our feet in the sun.
      Tinkle of porcelain on porcelain
    reminds us that even in peace,
there is struggle.
    No clam, razor, or moon
        wants to be destroyed
            in the tumultuous ride to freedom –
        to a new home
    because that is the ultimate goal
            in their strife.
Perfection is placed on polished shelves;
    trophies of victory for both sides.
        Some even find love for the damaged.
          Even a small hole and beautiful
    imperfections
        can bring colorful ceramic
          to our hearts. *J*

The Mermaid's Tears

She rests on a seaside rock,
forlorn, forsaken,
lost in thought,
surrounded by her frosted tears.
The graceful tilt of her head,
the curve of her spine,
her lower body half in the water.
Deceiving at first glance,
or is it?
Why is she crying?
Why such sadness in her eyes?
Will he speak to her?
Of course, I know he will.
His need to help overrules sanity.
She hears him approach,
quickly slides off the rock,
slips underwater without a sound,
and swims away with exquisite ease.
She turns to face him a
haunting smile on her lips.
She swims so far out
he can no longer see her.
He longs for her return.
He gathers her tears before he leaves.
Now he often sits on that rock
thinking of her.
From time to time
she leaves him sea glass gems
at the base of that rock
so he knows she's been there. £

My Daughter

My constant critic,
encouraging mentor,
computer consultant,
cohort in nonsense,
warming my heart,
my daughter,
sharing my zest for life,
standing tall,
daring to be different,
meeting life head on,
drifting toward a
subtle role reversal
that simultaneously
frightens me and consoles me,
but I smile
secure in her love,
affirmed in mine. £

My Mother

Creative cook
brilliant baker,
out of the kitchen
she is no risk taker.
Loves to talk
but lends an ear
when there is something
you want her to hear.
Always smiling
and ready to joke,
however there is a wrath
you don't want to evoke.
I can count on her
for valuable advice.
I'm so glad
she is in my life. *J*

The Seedy Chipmunk

The confident thief comes
in daylight. Cautiously,
he approaches the stash –
ears flicker as he is poised
to run if suspected.
There is no disguise –
no mask around his eyes
to hide his identity.
He studies the tiny gems
(rarities at this season),
reaches with his gloved hands,
and grabs a hold of the first
onyx oval. Where best to stow
these delicacies than one's mouth.
Greedily, the thief begins
to surpass his quota –
stuffing until his cheeks
bulge. So engrossed
in his sticky-fingered crime,
he didn't hear the observer
approach until a flash
caught his eye. His image
graces the front page –
"Wanted" with no place to hide. *J*

The Hummingbird

Feathered in thistle seeds,
her nest is her retreat,
her safe haven
when gale-like winds
overpower her
until she can resume
her favorite routes
to sup in thoraxes of salvia,
morning glories, and geraniums.
Her purpose is to bring joy,
or beauty, or pollen.
Perhaps it's just to be,
and to ensure those ongoing,
everlasting necessities in life
when her mini white
jelly-bean-like eggs hatch. £

The Spark

The little girl is handed a notebook,
a pencil, and a new world
where only her imagination
is the limit.
She writes a story about a cat
who accidentally sits on a firework.
She writes about Christmas
using words that were
provided to her.
She expanded her world
beyond plot using
rhyme and rhythm
to a poem of "Poor Grandpa."
Years ago
this little girl was given
a spark of possibilities
that ignited
under watchful eyes
and careful tending.
To this day, the girl's teacher
still observes,
gives feedback,
and is fully involved
in the pastime that she introduced
when the girl was just a child. *J*

Teacher

I have always been, and still am,
a learner and a teacher.
I crave learning new things,
it is as crucial to my life as the air I breathe
but more that,
I need to share what I have learned.
I need to show, tell, and inspire
so that nothing is lost,
so that everything is captured
in a letter, poem, or story
because smiles and caresses are too fleeting.
But every teacher needs a willing student.
One who wants to learn to tie a shoelace,
bake cookies, create a rhyme, build a bird house,
tempt appetites, dance, plant bulbs, sing songs,
notice sun rises and sun sets, and
hear the message in whispering winds.
One who understands posterity as I do.
One who is willing to take time
to work and rework
until it's the best it can be, and
then polish it to a fine glow.
One who shares the warmth
of heart and soul,
for humans are not instinctive,
we must learn
to nurture, hold dear, love,
and—we must teach. *L*

What Won't Kill You

Ladies and gents
gather round
for the next greatest invention
is what we have found.
In women's beauty
we have lipstick of lead,
and in the bakery
monodioxidine bread.
A dash of formaldehyde
in polish for nails,
and enough high fructose corn syrup
to make you grow frail.
The cell phone and laptops
come complete with Bing.
Just don't put them by
your "reproductive things."
Don't worry my sweets,
these are all tested and approved.
The fine print is you might need
a sixth finger removed. *J*

What Doesn't Kill You Makes You Stronger

The melody is upbeat,
the words so true;
facing your worse fear,
words so terrifying to hear,
yet hoping, praying, trying,
day by day, tear by tear.

Do not accept defeat,
faith will carry you through;
remember help is near,
this will be a special year,
stay focused on surviving,
then live your life with cheer. ℒ

Snow

Softly falling
kissing children's faces,
mothers calling
telling them to be careful.

Flake after flake
building upon each other,
adults reaching to take
shovels to push it all away.

Snow swishing
outside in the night,
children wishing
school will be closed.

Making the day
cool and dreadful,
melting away
when warmth arrives. *J*

Snowflake

Snowflake of white glazed porcelain,
six-sided complex nature,
simple exquisite reminder
symbolizing uniqueness
surprising individuality,
so apropos, so meaningful a gift,
simply worn on a golden chain. ℒ

Moving Plans

I've moved thirteen times
in seven states
and I hope that's all there is
for the road ahead.
I plan to stay at the beach,
and not move to a facility
before my final move to heaven.
I must admit, each move
was a positive step up.
I saw a lot of our country,
met wonderful people,
and have endearing memories.
So what's ahead for me?
This final quarter century
will be cherished as much
as all the others,
maybe even more so.
I will remain positive,
champion love and truth
as I have always done.
Once I get to heaven
I will continue to model myself
after my maternal grandmother
watching, guiding, and protecting
those I left on earth.
That sounds like a good plan. £

Change

I say goodbye to my friends
when my parents decide to move again.
I didn't have a say in it,
the journey never seems to end.

Some old "friends" are forgotten,
but many new ones are made.
I laugh as I think
maybe it's some kind of trade.

When I return to visit,
there's one thing many say:
"You've changed a lot!"
Let me ask you something, if I may.

Have I really changed?
Or could it be
that you never took the time
to get to know me? *J*

Jeweled Castles

Multi-colored jewels
glitter across the shore
exfoliating my feet
as I stroll –
shoes off
soles embraced
in nature's spa.
I bend down and pinch
a few granules
into my hand.
Peer closely –
one is a diamond,
another an onyx, two are emeralds
with a grey tiger's eye.
Different colors
with varying sizes
meld together
to create this
extravagant carpet.
It's no wonder these granules
construct castles. *J*

A Work of Art

Were I to peer
into a microscope at
a single grain of sand
I'd realize that
it's as unique
as each snowflake.

Each a microscopic
discovery of beauty
where least expected.

An infinite
number of grains
beneath my feet
as I walk the beach
and each one
a work of art. £

Depressed Memories

In my mind, there will always be February.
Your fingers float on the keys of the piano
and the melody dances after my mind and
erases thoughts of the coffin. We were in
a different country when we heard the news
and our sorrow illuminated us against
the background of joy. I dropped a lotus blossom
into the river – my symbol of remembrance.
Thoughts of broken promises mocked me
and I swore my mind was being burned
by a cinder. But we held each other and
continued looking ahead through wet lashes –
our despair was the only thing that kept us
together then, and caused us to never look back. *J*

Beginning of the End

The overcast day adds to
the sense of doom.
The piano player's
melancholy tune
accents her mood.
Sadness usually so deeply hidden
beneath her surface smile
seeks a level of release.
Pulse races.
Cool façade crumbles.
Composure deserts.
At first she laughed at
the foolishness of it all,
weeks of crying and agonizing.
Then she became concerned,
now she is scared.
When did it start?
What does it mean?
Why can't she shake it?
No diversions help.
She cannot bear anything else,
she cannot swallow
the lump in her throat
as she tries to keep tears
from spilling over
because
once that happens
she will not be able to stop. ℒ

A Poet

A poet plays with words,
rhymes them, counts them,
searches for the perfect one.

A poet is an artist
using colorful terms
that paint a picture for readers.
Each nuance of meaning,
each uttered sound,
each line carefully chosen
as a poet creates
using imagery or sensory cues.

A poet is a visionary
who writes in a new way,
literally, metaphorically, mystically;
expressions that engender curiosity
or a host of emotions.

A poet produces magic
with a creative arrangement
of simple words
that warm the heart
or heal the soul. £

Expansive Expression

Feel of paper
crinkle under my skin.
Scratch of lead
across the page.
Strength of wood
gripped between fingers.
Flick of the wrist
to scrawl the words.
Movement of the arm
composes a song.
Alternating alliteration
fills the verse. *J*

I'm Not Perfect

Blonde and beautiful
thin and tall
assails our vision
wherever we look.
TV and magazines
all around showing girls
what "beauty" is.
From a young age,
we are introduced to
make-up, domestication, body image.
Beauty is not a 00,
nor is it a hair color
or a "smoky eye" look.
Redefine beauty,
relook at your image.
We all have flaws,
some prefer to hide
rather than embrace.
Even an Angel's Trumpet
can be toxic on the inside. *J*

Senescence

She glides forward
with a bearing of
a former dancer.
Her gait belies her
inner turmoil.
Her secret fear
well hidden by
her aura of tranquility
often interpreted as
aloofness.
When she sees herself
in her mirror
she sees what
she wants to see.
But what do we see?
It doesn't really matter,
for she truly is love, grace,
and ageless. £

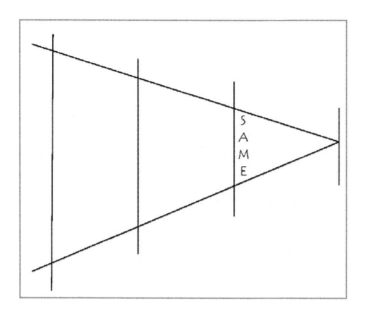

SAME captures topics that, to our surprise, turned out to be the same. We agreed to write about fruit only to later discover that we both wrote about peaches and both wrote it as a prose poem. We wrote about writing at the beach in "Secret Paradise" and "Treasures," and about photography, one about displaying them in "Photographs" and the other about time-lapsed photography in "Seeing the Unseen." Sometimes we assigned a subject just to see how each one would treat it. One of those assignments was "The Magic Box." More interestingly, we both wrote about our boyfriends, I wrote "My Love" in 1953 and updated it twice over the ensuing 60 years, and Jen wrote "My Beau" in 2012. When things like that started happening, we were pleased to learn that we were more alike than we thought even though almost 50 years separates us. It's a genetic thing that warms my heart and makes me smile. *L*

The Magic Box

I will put in the box
the tinkle of seashells surfing to shore,
the drumbeat of rain, the silence of snow,
the swish of taffeta ball gowns.

I will put in the box
the perfume of lilacs and freshly baked bread,
the taste of sizzling steaks and coconut drinks,
the contented hum of purring kittens.

I will put in the box
autumn breezes, fluttering ribbons,
every sunrise, Maui sunsets,
and my lover's kisses.

My box will be made of rainbows,
its magical contents interacting,
creating the wonderful music of life, and
distant vistas beyond simple pleasures.

I will keep my box in view,
refilling it from time to time,
thankful for these treasures
I gladly share with you. £

The Magic Box

I will put in my box
the music of favorite songs,
the feel of a summer breeze,
laughter of family reunions.

I will put in the box
the scent of roses,
perfect sunsets on a tropical isle,
shooting stars in a flawless night sky.

I will put in the box
the feelings of true love,
a child's wonder,
sounds of nature.

My box will be made of
moonbeams, love's first kiss,
and intellectual curiosity
seared together with the fire of dragons.

I will display my box
for everyone to see
and to remind myself
of the beauty in the world. J

Peaches

My favorite fruit is the peach. I love biting into one when it is perfectly ripe; allowing the juice to dribble down my chin. The soft fuzz on the outside brings joy to my fingertips and a smile dances on my lips. The scent is so refreshing that I buy soaps and sprays that have this delightful smell. Even the word "peach" is used in relation to one who is sweet. The taste reminds me of summer. I infuse it into chicken and salads and use the flavor to brighten my drinks – tea, juice, and martinis. If I am ever in need of a pick-me-up, this delectable fruit always does the trick. *J*

Peaches

The lush shape, downy skin, pleasing scent, and juicy insides make me salivate just thinking of them. Fresh picked peaches still warm from the sun are *the* best. Eight peach trees in our backyard yielded nine years of peach treats. Song birds nesting in those trees delighted us. I was in awe one winter morning when our peach trees were covered with ice after a storm. Those bare-branched trees became a crystal wonderland glistening in the sunlight. Despite that harsh winter the faithful, gnarled trees blessed us with their bounty the next summer. Whenever I eat peach ice cream, it makes me think it's summertime even when it isn't. I like knowing peaches are my grand-daughter's favorite fruit. £

Secret Paradise

Follow the sound of the waves, and the scent of flowers. Here lies my secret paradise. While sitting on rocks, I soak in the sunshine that bathes my face. The weather is warm with a refreshing breeze. Shorebirds cheerfully chirp. The sand and cool water caress my feet as I watch the waves break against stone. There's a hammock strung across two trees. At night, you can actually see the stars dusting a blanket of black. I sip an iced latte and drift away into my thoughts, inspired by the serene beauty around me. I pull out a pen and paper, creativity surging, and begin to write. *J*

Treasures

Blue-green gem
crashing at my feet.
Eternal beauty
shared with vocal shorebirds
as I search for sea treasures
tossed up by foaming surf.
Salty sea sprays
season my thoughts
and I write about everything
that comes to mind,
people, places, paradigms,
especially treasured memories
of times long past,
so precious
they sustain me yet. £

Seeing the Unseen

I catch my breath
as wonders unfold.
Captivated,
I see the unseen.
Buds blossoming,
hummingbirds dining,
eggs hatching,
soufflés rising.
Those visions
awaken my mind as I see
the origin of a smile,
and countless possibilities
to look for,
to find, and to
see the unseen. *L*

Photographs

Pictures are all over,
each one holds a memory.
A memory of an event,
of feelings and stages.
Examine one and a
mental movie begins.
It's amazing what
details are remembered,
and how many are forgotten.
You can wrack your brain;
try to remember,
but even if you do,
some parts would be false.
So all we have are
these photographs
that we hang up
or store away.
Sooner or later they
will get picked up and
a story may get told.
Usually it's the flood of memories
that may or may not be true,
but we still believe. *J*

Diet

Is there a woman out there
who has not been on a diet?
Speak up, it's time to share.

Is there someone who doesn't care
who dreads the word diet?
Consider menus a nightmare.

Is this a lifetime cross we bear
to be ever watchful of our diet?
Counting points, carbs, calories in our fare.

Until the day we wake up and say
good-bye diet!
Let the pounds fall where they may. £

Diet

Low calorie
Fat free
Gluten free
Low sugar
Whole wheat.
Altered foods for an altered life.
What is the point of
dairy-free ice cream?
Or chocolate without sugar?
Our bodies cannot digest
fake foods with
chemically created ingredients.
What happened to self restraint?
What happened to the days
when a burger was a burger
and not ground beef
with meal filler
and hormone injections?
No thank you!
I'll stick to a natural diet
with a healthy dose
of exercise. *J*

What Is That?

What is that white disk
half-hidden behind
the sapphire screen?
A semi-circle curve
of a white beach ball
under a cerulean towel?
The top of a snowball
behind a navy mitten?
A white button peeking
through a buttonhole
on a royal coat?
A white dish half-covered
with a blue napkin?
A white marble?
A Necco wafer?
A spotlight?

No, it's the top of the
moon rising above
the midnight sea
to the deep blue sky.
As awe-inspiring
as any fiery sunset,
sometimes more so.
Cool white majestic drama
against serene shades
of blue, so beautiful like a
soul rising to heaven. £

Moon

The moon –
glorious,
beautiful,
inspiring.
I look up at it –
tonight with a new purpose.
Perhaps you are looking, too.
Though you are gone,
my heart holds you.
If you are looking,
the moon can be
our connection. *J*

Life

Ain't it funny –
this thing we call life.
So many not living,
traveling blindly,
and hoping to get it right.
Never enough time
never enough money
never enough possessions.
Rush around –
nose in phone.
Look up
see the sunset
the good deed
the life traveling by.
No stopping
no reflection –
and you wonder
where the time goes.
Blink
you're 81
and you've never lived. *J*

Life

I used to think
if I sauntered
through life,
I'd be okay.
But now I know
if I don't want to
stand in line
waiting to get into
heaven,
I'd better take control
of my direction.

So I did.
And then I learned
to rethink that direction,
tweak it now and then,
fine-tune it to
achieve satisfaction.
For now, all is well,
I am on schedule,
willing to make
adjustments
as necessary for
fulfillment. ℒ

My Beau

Eyes that sparkle in the daylight hours
look upon me with chocolate delight.
He cooks for me but has yet to bring me flowers,
with a glance or caress my heart takes flight.

I stand on my toes to receive a kiss,
my fingers run through strands of midnight silk.
We barely fight – it seems nothing is amiss,
sun-kissed and golden contrasts my skin of milk.

Serious debates followed by laughter and jest,
his ambitions and goals are ones I admire.
He returns me to sanity when I'm a mess.
I had no clue this love would transpire.

Scent of his cologne fills my heart to the brim,
but sometimes I need a vacation from him. *J*

My Love

Like distant deeps or summer skies—his eyes.
Like fields of wheat or streams of gold—his hair.

Behold—my love.

Like stormy spring or quiet winter—his face.
And oh the wonder in his warm embrace.

His loving heart, his tender kiss—all this

Behold—my love!

Addendum 33 years later:

Well, his eyes are still blue
and the love is still new,
but his blond hair is now white.
And the man?
The man is still pure delight!

Update 20 years later:

Well, true is true!
Bill, it's still wonderful
to love you and
be loved by you. *L*

The Monster

It was barely visible
as it had learned to blend in
to its surroundings at a young age,
ever so slowly spreading its limbs
as time passed.
It made its home among sandy dunes
that seemed to stretch for miles.
Some hide amongst the cracks
in clay and mud.
Perhaps it wouldn't get noticed –
not for a few days, at least.
Perhaps whoever saw it
would deny its existence
(they're only figments of our imagination).
Children constantly point them out,
but they are hushed
and no one looks to see if the truth is being told.
But eventually you would have to believe;
adults can't keep pretending
that age-old tales won't creep up on them.
And once one shows up,
it begins to multiply
like rabbits.
Slowly at first,
but eventually you blink
and they are all over the place.
Then you would have to believe
and the mirror never lies. *J*

Aging

When did I grow old?
Was it yesterday?
Why is my hair grey?
How did that happen?
What's that ringing noise?
Okay so vision is dimmer,
hearing so-so,
scent and taste are gone,
hands sizzle, and feet get numb.
Yet in my mind I am young.
So who is that old woman in my mirror?
I am young at heart
and forward thinking,
but my voice is raspy
my gait is slow and painful,
my skin is wrinkled.
Yet I still need to sing and dance
and embrace romance
even though my joints scream when I move,
and my heart thunders with little provocation.
Age may be just a number,
but have I grown old as well?
No, no, no, that cannot be.
Talk with me and you will see
that although I inhabit this aging body
my spirit is ageless.
So pop the cork, sip champagne, and
celebrate because I am here today
and so are you. *L*

Advice

I'm here to say
that this day
is the way
I need it to be.
Perhaps you'll agree
and learn to see
joy in simple things
as each day brings
reasons to sing.
Don't regulate
thoughts that frustrate,
trust in fate.
Worries may be rife.
Banish strife.
Choose to live life. £

Advice

Some advice from me to you
is not to order that pie.
I know you are wondering
so I'll tell you why.

You had some raccoon eyes
served to you on that plate,
and I can assure you,
you did eat all eight.

And I know what you ate
in that very bowl.
It was a nicely cooked
medium rare mole.

And in that glass
you drank liquid mice.
and I'm pretty sure
you had it refilled twice.

So now do you think
you want to order that pie?
I didn't think so,
now here's your check, goodbye! *J*

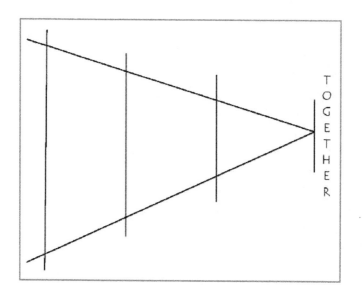

TOGETHER is the shortest chapter, but it was the most interesting to us. We searched our files to find the earliest poems that we wrote together, and eliminated the ones that were too juvenile, but saved them for a children's book. When I read "How Sweet It Is" to Jen in 1994, she liked the silliness of it, and that's how "Sundae" evolved; it was one of our first poems just for the fun of the images it conjured. We wrote it when Jen was eight years old, all in one session at the kitchen table, laughing at our nonsensical images. There were a few times during the course of writing this book when we didn't agree on a word or thought, but we managed to work it out as necessary. We wrote "Enchanted Garden" during and after our trip to Ireland. Now we write via e-mails; that's how "Dreams" and the other poems in this last section were written. This particular kind of interaction is fun and precious for both of us. £

Sundae

I think I'll make a sundae
with three scoops of snow,
a splash of bluebird feathers,
a spoonful of chopped crayons,
a dollop of clouds,
a sprinkle of ants,
topped with an acorn.
I'll make it in a silver dish and
use a magic spoon
for each delicious bite,
whenever I eat one spoonful
two more will appear so
my dish is never empty.
It often overflows on to
a round paper table,
melting before it hits
the crooked floor where
it runs across the room,
out the open door,
forming a rainbow river
deep enough for candy boats
and watermelon fish that
robot cats want to catch
before they fly away to a
purple moon that will
explode when they land
sending them to the bottom of
the sea where they might like to be
because the seashells
are happy to see them.
Tomorrow I'll make a Mondae. *LJ*

Dreams

Cross the threshold of consciousness
to the realm of fantasy
where cares are resolved and
worries are forgotten.

Dwell in this special place
to solve a riddle that
exposes unknown facts
or keys to the future.

Heed the lessons revealed
be a better person
know everything is okay
be happy, stay focused, proceed. *LJ*

The Written Word

The written word is a pleasure,
a skill I truly treasure.
I use it in full measure
as it helps to reassure
that my reasoning is pure
and that I will endure
despite ups and downs
that keep me tightly wound
until verbs, adjectives, nouns
dance across the page
like ballerinas on a stage.
My mind becomes uncaged
as I embrace the written word. *LJ*

Enchanted Garden

Moss lined garden paths,
a crystal waterfall impels
like a siren's call.

Hummingbirds and
butterflies abound, yet
neither makes a sound.

Mini rainbows arc as I
dive into a pool
so cool, so dark.

Impact causes water lilies
to parade, as droplets
dance and cascade.

Ruby roses and orchids of
pearl like lollypops in a
red and white swirl.

Weeping willows bend, a
bench is waiting
at the end.

Sunlit cobwebs as delicate
as lace, peace in this
enchanted place.

Entering is a bit of
heaven, leaving seems
unforgiven. *LJ*

Water

Often taken for granted,
this essential element
is 70 percent of the Earth's surface.
Yet it is as precious
as nurturing amniotic fluid
that cradles unborn children
in utero.
We see it often in liquid form
in rain, in seas, or coming from a tap.
Flowing gently
like the kiss of a moth
or cutting through mountains
like a powerful knife.
We know it in its gas form
in vapor and steam,
in clouds and fog.
We love it in its solid form
as ice to skate on
or to cool drinks and
clink in our glasses.
As snowflakes
that fall from the sky
in perfect imperfection.
Truly a gift,
water must be cherished,
not taken for granted.
Though it is abundant today,
you never know
when it could just
disappear. *LJ*

Grace

Pink and white petals
waltzing to the wind,
silent messengers
of all that might have been,
swirl around a ballerina
pirouetting by a lake
as she moves in a
fluid dreamlike state.
Hands folded with
interwoven fingers
holding tight to
memories that linger.
Bowed heads
before a simple feast
Acquiescence
in the name of peace. *LJ*

Chopsticks

Resist
    the urge to pierce food
Coordinate
    mind and fingers
Practice
    with a piece of chicken.
Once proficient
    try a grain of rice.

How odd is that?
When in the natural order
we start small and become large.

Try different methods
    grab
    scoop
    shish-ka-bob.
Each effort produces
few results
causing prolonged dinners.

Try again
food falls off
as it approaches your mouth
leaving nothing.
Patience is demanded.

There is only one
correct technique.
Practice will make you proficient.
Then think beyond eating
make the mind body connection.

With two index fingers
and the upper right side
of the keyboard.
Only seven notes
and you are done.

Why is a beginner's song
named after a device
that takes so long
to master?

I cannot think of that
as music to dine by.
Although practice is mandatory
to become adept
in both endeavors.

The real lesson learned is
have patience
and practice for success. *LJ*

Puzzles

A picture can have
a thousand pieces
with one unifying concept.
Match the gaps to make it cohesive.
Intense concentration, a good eye for detail,
spectrum of color and patterns are clues.
Start with a straight edge,
enlist help if you must.

Perplexities abound;
the unknown intrigues.
Construct an outline
before filling in the gaps.
Frame the bigger picture
with goals and wisdom.
Advice from sages
regarding fulfillment.
Trials and tribulations.
good times and bad.
The last piece often wanders away
only to be "found" after a day.
Who had it?
That's a puzzle within a puzzle. *LJ*

Silk

Soft and luxurious against my skin
gleaming crimson chiffon
winding like a scarlet river
to the moonlit crescent falls.
As I sway in the mist
the spangled fringe sings to me
like the soft spring rain
as it hits each leaf
in the canopy above.
A refreshing breeze catches
the edge of the silk
and unwinds it from my body.
A final twirl releases it –
floating through the air
and I am free.
I dive into the churning water
and allow the current
to carry me safely to an eddy.
Floating on my back,
I look out to the cosmos
and realize how vast the universe is.
A flash of red silk cascades
through the night sky
carrying my worries away. *LJ*

Earth

Mysterious
marble with swirled
white ribbons over green,
brown, and tan land masses
in a sea of velvety blue ripples.
A home for all God's creatures.
An orb suspended among the
stars from the Milky Way,
so breathtaking serene.
Beautiful gem of the
Universe. *LJ*

Conclusion

So ends our poetry efforts. We loved the experience and found out a lot more about each other. We hope you found our approach to poetry entertaining. Some of it was easy to understand, others may have required reading between the lines, so-to-speak, and still others may make you wonder what we were writing about. Nevertheless, if you enjoyed it, then we accomplished our mission. *£*

Something to Think About has been years in the writing; we are excited to finally share it with you. Writing together allowed us to see different perspectives on our work and on the subject matter in general. It forced us to look beyond our initial interpretations and continue to grow as writers. We encourage you to find a way to connect with your grandparent/grandchild in an experience that will undoubtedly bring you closer together. *J*

Jen and I look forward to working together on another book someday, perhaps a book of fiction stories. With that in mind, I want to tell you about one snowy day during the winter of 2010. The Washington D.C. area was snowed-in by a three-day snowstorm and Jen was housebound by a whiteout. I was in sunny Florida at the time and decided to keep her company for a while. I proposed the idea that we write a story together just as we did poetry and juvenile stories long ago. Jen liked the idea. So, with no plot, no character assignments, no specific setting in mind, three days of e-mail started, and a fine story evolved.

I wrote the first paragraph, she wrote the next. I wrote from the young woman's perspective, Jen wrote from an older woman's perspective. It was interesting that she chose a name starting with L for her character and I chose one starting with J for my character—an unplanned occurrence, by the way. It's no surprise that the beach was our setting.

After the first draft, the story sat in limbo for a long time. We worked on it sporadically during the next few months, often slipping into the other character's voice; it was good to be that flexible and that in-tune with each other's thought processes. Every now and then we'd discuss some details, what would work, and what wouldn't. As I entered changes in the rewrites, there were times when I really did not know which words were Jen's and which were mine. Either way, we have *no regrets*. We offer this fiction story to you. *L*

No Regrets

Jean liked to park her car near the beach access point on Spinnaker Road whenever she brown-bagged her lunch. Away from the office din, she could breathe the moist salty air and allow the surf sounds to work their magic. This was her favorite hour of the day. There were usually several cars here on weekdays, but today hers was the only one. As she unpacked her salad she heard the crunch of footsteps on the hard-packed shell road.

A glance in her rear view mirror told her that it was no one she knew. An older lady she had never seen before was strolling toward the beach with a plastic bag in hand. A sunhat rested on top of her graying bob and sunglasses covered nearly half of her face. Jean watched as the woman walked past her and onto the fine sandy beach. She became intrigued when the woman walked straight to the shoreline and stood motionless as she let the ocean lap at her feet.

Five minutes had passed before the woman moved. Jean finished her lunch but continued to watch as the woman opened the plastic bag and took out what looked like a dome-shaped wooden box. Sunlight glinted off the brass findings on the box as she caressed the lid. Jean felt like a voyeur, but she couldn't take her eyes away from the woman who seemed oblivious of the water soaking the hem of her slacks. She seemed to sway as she pulled the box closer to her midsection. After a while she looked down at the box as if she'd never seen it before. She tilted her head slightly and continued to sway in a rhythmic manner. It only took a few seconds for Jean to realize that the woman was dancing. A small box step, it appeared.

When she was finished, she slowly lifted the lid of the box and held it out to the ocean, almost as an offering to some distant sea god. As the woman opened the top of the box, a gust of wind blew the contents out. They fluttered across the water like a flock of plovers startled from of their sand nests frantically escaping over the sea. On closer inspection Jean saw that they were torn pieces of paper.

Love letters from a lover long gone, Jean surmised. *Why? Why would she throw letters away? Was the woman obliterating her past, destroying evidence of a lover, or paying homage to a special person in her life?* Jean decided that she had to talk to the woman. She opened her car door, took off her Jimmy Choos, and walked to the edge of the sand. Not wanting to startle the old woman Jean called out, "Excuse me, ma'am."

The woman continued to stare ahead as the pieces of paper came to rest in the water and drifted out to sea. Jean continued to stand behind the woman, not wanting to interrupt whatever ceremony was occurring. The woman eventually spoke.

"Come beside me, dear," she said in a soft, yet firm voice.

Jean approached silently.

"Watching this whole time, were you?" the woman finally asked. Jean froze, wondering if she had intruded in any way.

"Why, yes," she stammered, "but I didn't mean to."

"Then you must have questions." The woman finally cast a glance at Jean, but quickly returned her gaze to the horizon. "Ask away."

"Well, I don't want to be intrusive or nosey. Are you okay?"

"Oh, yes. There comes a time in life when you have to let go of the past. Actually, I've clung to these letters way too long. It's not healthy to dwell on the past. I may be old and sentimental, but a realist nonetheless."

"May I ask what the letters were about? An old love?" Jean asked.

"Isn't that always what they're about?" the woman asked with a wry smile. "Yes, they were from a life long ago."

"Forgive my questions, but why did you finally decide to get rid of the letters?"

The woman looked at Jean for a long while. So long, in fact, that Jean thought she had gone too far. Right when she was about to apologize, the woman spoke. "What is your name?"

"Jean," she responded, a bit taken aback. "How rude of me; I should have introduced myself. May I ask your name?"

"Lorraine," the woman responded. "Before I answer your questions, Jean, I want to ask you one of my own. Why do you care what an old woman might be doing?"

119

"If you knew me, you'd know I care about everything. I thought you were performing a ritual, especially when you started to dance. That intrigued me. When you tossed the letters out it seemed so sad and so final. I thought you might need someone with you. No one should be all alone at a time like that."

"You're so kind, Jean, but I assure you I am perfectly fine. As I said, these letters are from long ago. I have moved on since then, but a part of me could never let go of the letters. Until now."

"What happened between you two?" Jean asked, still wanting answers but unsure if she was probing too much.

Lorraine sighed and looked out to sea again. "It's quite a long story. History, really. I don't want to bore you with my past."

"You wouldn't bore me, I am the one who is probably asking too many questions," Jean replied.

Lorraine chuckled to herself.

"I do not mind. It actually might be nice to get this off my chest. I haven't told anyone this story, not even my daughter, so I suppose it's about time." Lorraine paused still looking out to sea.

Jean looked on, wondering what story this woman had to tell that she would keep hidden for all these years.

"Okay, but I'll tell you the short version. Let's move up to one of those benches behind the dunes."

When they had settled themselves Jean asked, "Sure you want to tell all?"

"Of course! Almost 40 years ago, I was healthy and wild and in love with life. My job took me all over the world. I traveled extensively and loved extensively as well. But exciting as all that was, I knew something was missing from my life. Maybe it was my biological clock reminding me that it was time to settle down. But the man I was seeing at the time wasn't interested in being domesticated. So we parted our ways and I came back to the States. Maybe I shouldn't have given him an ultimatum, but I was a bit of a drama queen back then."

"And the letters?" Jean prompted.

"The letters started arriving two or three a week at first. Then they tapered off. Each one begged me to reconsider my decision. Each one promised me a life full of excitement, but with no mention of a marriage proposal. After several weeks, I stopped reading them and just tossed them in the bottom drawer of my desk."

"How long did you continue to get letters?"

"Oh, just for another month or so. I never answered them and didn't read most of them. I made up my mind to change my lifestyle and eventually focus on finding a suitable mate."

"And did you?"

"Yes, I certainly did! I met a fine gentleman in my art class."

"An artist!"

"No, he was just a dabbler like me. We went out for coffee after class once in a while and a comfortable friendship developed which eventually evolved into a romance. We married during the second year of our *friendship*. And it's been wonderful."

"Such a lovely story! Do you have any other children besides your daughter?"

"No, I didn't have any children with him."

"But, your daughter. . ."

"Ah, yes, my daughter—my love child."

An awkward moment or two passed. "Does she know?"

"Not really. I mean she knows my husband isn't her father. She was three when I married him. But I didn't tell her much about her birth father except that he had died. I don't want to debate the right or wrong aspects of my decision. It's the way I needed it to be."

"Did you ever tell your lover about the child?"

"No. I didn't want to force him into marriage just because I was pregnant. It was all for the best. He was spoiled, egotistical, and a bit strange. I sometimes wonder how I had ever fit into his life."

"So, no regrets?"

"None! I've had a fantastic life and I'm very much in love with my husband. I was long overdue to get rid of those sappy letters."

"Did you ever read any of the unopened ones?"

"You know, I thought about doing that, but then I realized it really didn't matter. I had put that part of my life away forever. No sense unsettling the apple cart, so to speak. So I came here today to bid farewell to those memories. Period! End of the story."

"Well, thank you for sharing your story with me, Lorraine. I've taken a very long lunch hour today and I'd better get back to my office."

"Okay, my dear. It was so nice being with you. Thank you for listening to an old woman ramble."

"You are welcome. I enjoyed being with you as well. Where do you live, Lorraine? Do you need a lift?"

"That's a lovely offer, but I think I would enjoy the stroll home. We're renting a cottage just up the road, so once I knew we'd be by the shore, I packed the letters into my suitcase. I still enjoy a bit of theatrics now and then, and thought this seemed like an appropriate way to dispose of them with flair."

We said our good-byes once again, shared a hug, and parted. *LJ*

CPSIA information can be obtained
at www.ICGtesting.com
Printed in the USA
LVOW04s2246181215

467182LV00003B/3/P